ISAAC ASIMOV'S NEW LIBRARY OF THE UNIVERSE

MODERN ASTRONOMY

BY ISAAC ASIMOV
WITH REVISIONS AND UPDATING BY GREG WALZ-CHOJNACKI

Gareth Stevens Publishing
MILWAUKEE

For a free color catalog describing Gareth Stevens' list of high-quality books, call 1-800-542-2595 (USA) or 1-800-461-9120 (Canada). Gareth Stevens' Fax: (414) 225-0377.

Library of Congress Cataloging-in-Publication Data

Asimov, Isaac.
  Modern astronomy / by Isaac Asimov; with revisions and updating
by Francis Reddy.
    p. cm. — (Isaac Asimov's New library of the universe)
  Rev. ed. of: Astronomy today. 1990.
  Includes index.
  Summary: Offers an account of how scientists and amateurs use
instruments such as space telescopes, computers, radio telescopes,
and binoculars to study the universe.
  ISBN 0-8368-1236-0
  1. Astronomy—Observers' manuals—Juvenile literature.
[1. Astronomy.] I. Walz-Chojnacki, Greg, 1954-. II. Asimov, Isaac.
Astronomy today. III. Title. IV. Series: Asimov, Isaac. New library
of the universe.
QB64.A74 1996
520—dc20   95-40380

This edition first published in 1996 by
Gareth Stevens Publishing
1555 North RiverCenter Drive, Suite 201
Milwaukee, Wisconsin 53212, USA

Revised and updated edition © 1996 by Gareth Stevens, Inc.
Original edition published in 1990 by Gareth Stevens, Inc.,
under the title *Astronomy Today*. Text © 1996 by Nightfall, Inc.
End matter and revisions © 1996 by Gareth Stevens, Inc.

Project editor: Barbara J. Behm
Design adaptation: Helene Feider
Editorial assistant: Diane Laska
Production director: Teresa Mahsem
Picture research: Matthew Groshek and Diane Laska

Printed in the United States of America

1 2 3 4 5 6 7 8 9 99 98 97 96

To bring this classic of young people's information up to date, the editors at Gareth Stevens Publishing have selected two noted science authors, Greg Walz-Chojnacki and Francis Reddy. Walz-Chojnacki and Reddy coauthored the recent book *Celestial Delights: The Best Astronomical Events Through 2001*.

Walz-Chojnacki is also the author of the book *Comet: The Story Behind Halley's Comet* and various articles about the space program. He was an editor of *Odyssey*, an astronomy and space technology magazine for young people, for eleven years.

Reddy is the author of nine books, including *Halley's Comet, Children's Atlas of the Universe, Children's Atlas of Earth Through Time*, and *Children's Atlas of Native Americans*, plus numerous articles. He was an editor of *Astronomy* magazine for several years.

CONTENTS

We live in an enormously large place – the Universe. It's just in the last fifty-five years or so that we've found out how large it probably is. It's only natural that we would want to understand the place in which we live, so scientists have developed instruments – such as radio telescopes, satellites, probes, and many more – that have told us far more about the Universe than could possibly be imagined.

We have seen planets up close. We have learned about quasars and pulsars, black holes, and supernovas. We have gathered amazing data about how the Universe may have come into being and how it may end. Nothing could be more astonishing.

Modern astronomy makes use of large and complex instruments of many kinds—but it is practiced in simpler ways, as well. Astronomy is a science in which all people—young and not-so-young, amateur and professional—can participate. Even with basic instruments, such as binoculars and telescopes, the Universe is open to everyone!

Isaac Asimov

Gazing Skyward

In ancient times, astronomers simply gazed skyward to make their discoveries. Without any special tools, they learned a great deal about the Sun, Moon, and planets. They also determined the length of a year and developed calendars.

Today, astronomers still observe the sky. But they have new ways of gathering information and new ideas about how the Universe works. For example, modern astronomers use instruments that can collect vast amounts of light and that study the kinds of radiation that are invisible to the eye. Astronomers today also use modern technology to determine such things as how stars came to be, how they change with time, and how they will come to an end.

Opposite: A misty path called the Milky Way cuts through the darkness of the night sky. The Milky Way is the combined light of billions of stars.
Inset: The human eye detects only visible light, but scientific instruments reveal radiation beyond the red and violet ends of the visible spectrum.

Below, top: A South Korean postage stamp celebrates an ancient observatory.

Below, bottom: The Medicine Wheel at Big Horn, Wyoming, was an ancient observatory used to record the motions of celestial objects and, like a calendar, to measure the passing of the days.

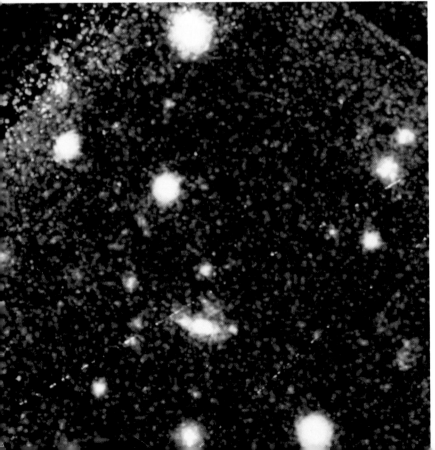

Above: When the Keck "twins" are both working, astronomers will have a colossal pair of "binoculars" with which to make exciting new discoveries.

Left: The first Keck telescope took this photograph of the most distant known galaxy. Imagine what the Keck "binoculars" will see!

Opposite, top: Workers polish one of Keck's mirrors.

Opposite, bottom: The 200-inch (5-m) telescope on Palomar Mountain in California.

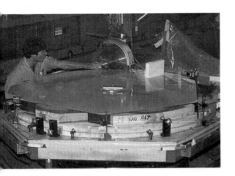

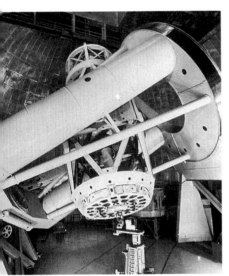

New Eyes on the Sky

For years, the great 200-inch (5-meter) telescope on Palomar Mountain in California was the largest telescope on Earth. In recent years, however, scientists have been using new methods to build much larger telescopes.

On the Hawaiian mountain of Mauna Kea, a 400-inch (10-m) telescope, the Keck Telescope, has begun making exciting new observations of the Universe. A second, identical scope is being built next to it. By 1996, the Keck Telescope will have a twin. These two telescopes will be linked by computer to act as one – a telescope four times bigger than the Palomar "giant!"

The Keck telescopes will have 36 smaller mirrors combined into one huge mirror. This sounds complicated, but it is much easier to accomplish than manufacturing one huge mirror.

! ***The new telescopes – getting a bead on the cosmos!***

Scientists are building better telescopes for use on the ground and in the air. In the telescopes, a vacuum is applied to one side of a mirror. The mirror is then "sprung" into contact with air, where it takes on an appropriate shape. High above, flying observatories sail the skies. These specially equipped planes help astronomers view the Sun, planets, and even distant stars from high above the distortion of Earth's atmosphere. More than ever, our "eyes" are on the stars.

A Clear Picture

It doesn't matter whether the telescope you use is in an observatory or in your bedroom window – there will be times when visibility will be poor. Clouds and fog can hide the sky. The atmosphere can absorb and scatter light so you cannot see the stars. Even on clear nights, the air can be unsteady, causing the stars to "quiver."

Even the Hubble Space Telescope has experienced problems with visibility. Hubble, launched in 1990, promised to revolutionize astronomy with crystal clear views of the cosmos. Unfortunately, there was a defect in its mirror, and the first pictures weren't as sharp as expected.

But Hubble was designed with repairs in mind. And in 1993, astronauts repaired the great orbiting observatory. Astronomers are now using it to study some of the many mysteries of the Universe.

Opposite: Astronaut Jeff Hoffman installs a new camera in the Hubble Space Telescope.

Below: These photos show how Hubble's repairs cleared up its blurry vision.

Bottom: Observatories are often built on mountaintops, where telescopes can look through the clean, dry air above the clouds.

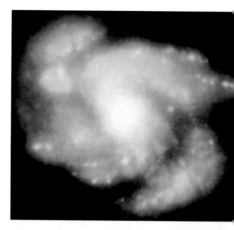

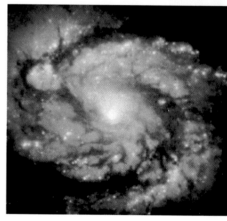

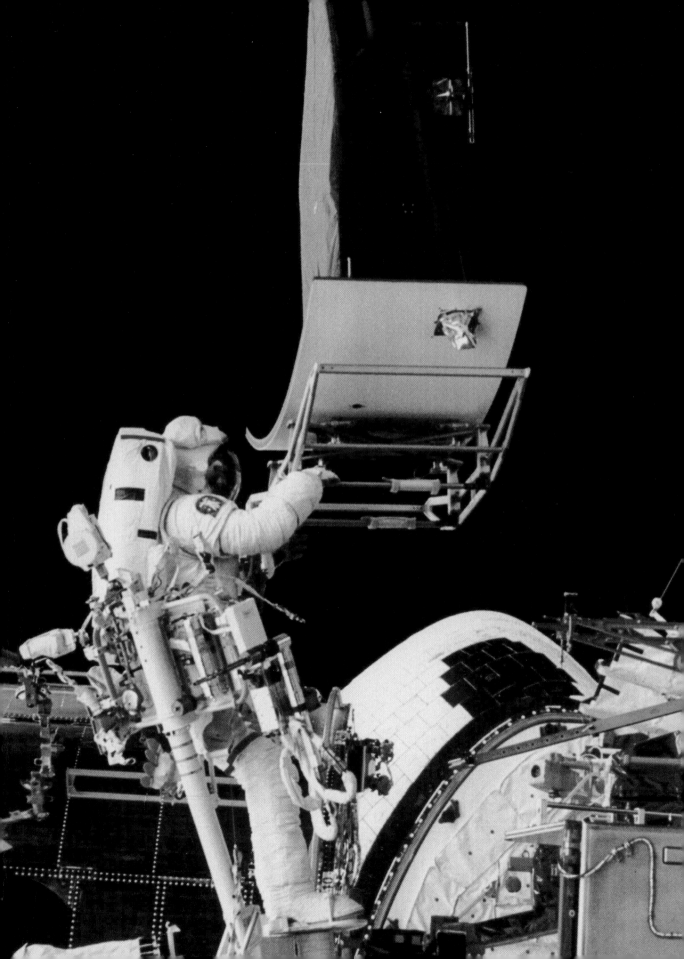

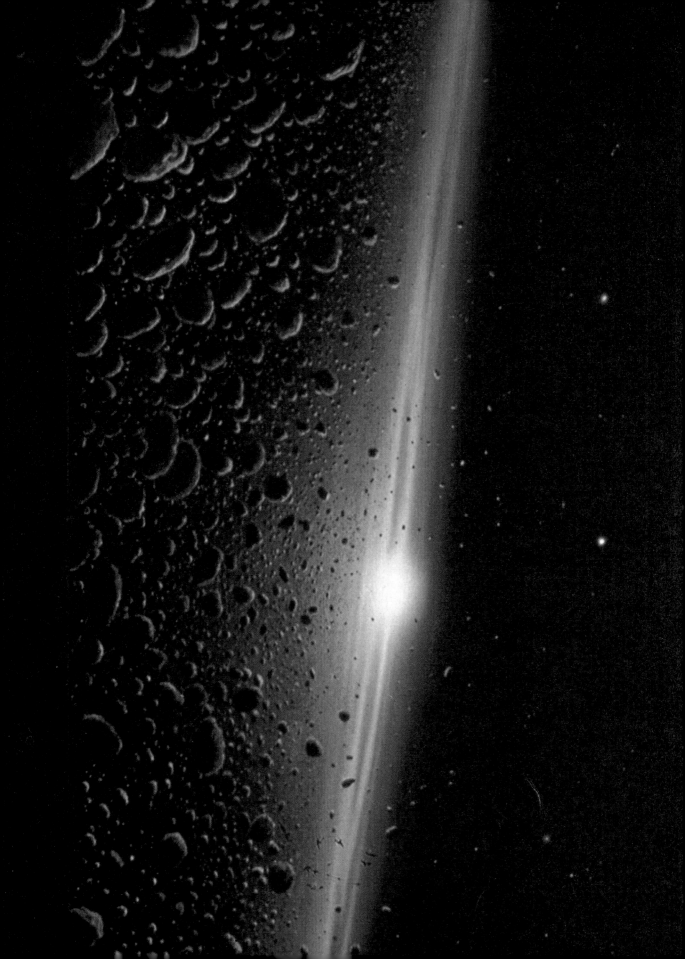

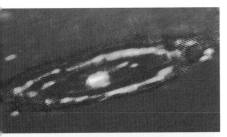

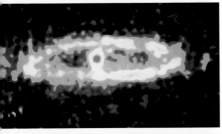

Listening to the Radio . . . Waves!

Stars give off radio waves as well as light, and special radio telescopes have been built that receive and concentrate radio waves.

Radio waves transmit certain information that light does not. For example, radio waves have helped astronomers detect very distant objects called quasars and tiny, rapidly rotating stars called pulsars. Black holes in the center of galaxies and various chemicals in clouds of dust between stars have been discovered by radio waves.

In addition, a satellite called the Infrared Astronomical Satellite (IRAS) has detected heat waves called infrared waves. IRAS recently picked up infrared waves in the area of distant stars. These signals may mean that planets are forming around the stars.

Would you believe . . . Little Green Men!

In 1967, a British astronomer, Jocelyn Bell Burnell, helped develop a huge radio telescope made of 2,048 antennae. Radio signals detected by this telescope were so steady that scientists wondered if the signals came from an intelligent source. The signals were called LGM, for "Little Green Men." But they were too steady to be of intelligent origin. Bell Burnell had discovered pulsars – rapidly spinning neutron stars that send out radio signals with each turn.

Opposite: Are planets forming around the star Beta Pictoris? Many astronomers believe that a cloud of dust and gas, similar to that which made our Solar System, encircles the star.

Above: M31, the closest spiral galaxy to Earth – as seen by infrared *(top)*, radio waves *(center)*, and visible light *(bottom)*.

Left: Dr. Jocelyn Bell Burnell discovered pulsars.

The Superscope Age

Scientists use computers to join a number of small telescopes into one large telescope. In this way, radio telescopes that are perhaps thousands of miles apart combine and become more powerful than any single telescope.

Computers can also analyze the light that telescopes receive and study it with greater precision than the human eye or cameras can. Thanks to computers, astronomers can now see dim stars, remote galaxies, and other distant objects in the sky more sharply than ever before.

Opposite: An array of small radio telescopes can be joined by computer to function as one giant "superscope."

Inset: An astronomer studies an image produced by a combination of radio telescopes.

Below: The Very Large Array collection of radio telescopes in Socorro, New Mexico. Each arm of the VLA is 13 miles (21 km) long.

Right: A network of radio telescopes could be linked to create a massive antenna.

Distant Lights

As scientists view objects that are farther and farther off in space, they also see them as they existed longer and longer ago.

Traveling at about 186,000 miles (300,000 kilometers) per second, light from the nearest star (other than our Sun) takes over four years to reach Earth. Light from two "nearby" galaxies, the Magellanic clouds, takes over 150,000 years to reach Earth. Light from the Andromeda Galaxy, another galactic neighbor, takes over 2 million years to arrive on Earth.

Quasars are distant objects with very bright centers. They can be seen from Earth by light that left them 1-10 billion years ago. The most advanced scientific instruments can see galaxies by light that left them 17 billion years ago.

These astronomical figures reveal something about how old the Universe might be – and the way it developed after its birth.

Opposite: A diver works inside a water-filled device known as a particle detector. Within the detector, over two thousand light sensors watch for the telltale flashes that occur when particles called neutrinos are captured. This is important because minutes before astronomers' instruments detected supernova 1987A, a smattering of neutrinos given off by the dying star passed through particle detectors.

Inset: A computer shows which sensors detect a flash from a passing neutrino.

Below: Supernova 1987A *(the bright spot on the left)* in the Large Magellanic Cloud.

! *A "neighborly" supernova – 1987A!*

Every once in a great while, a star explodes into a super-nova and briefly shines with the light of a billion ordinary stars. Not since 1604 has a supernova appeared in our Galaxy. But in 1987, a supernova occurred in the Large Magellanic Cloud, a neighboring galaxy to our Milky Way. At last, astronomers could study a supernova that was fairly close at hand.

A Worthwhile Watch

Being an astronomer may sound like fun, but it is also very hard work. It may mean staying up all night to observe the skies and spending countless hours examining data for days, weeks, and even months on end.

Besides astronomers, there are others who keep watch on the skies. Technicians operate the scopes, handle the cameras, develop the films, analyze the light, and perform other related tasks.

What's more, in order to "see" above the thickest, dirtiest part of Earth's atmosphere, most large telescopes are on mountains. And because heating an observatory can make the air quiver and distort the image in a scope, astronomers often work in the cold night air.

But keep in mind that the excitement of making a new, important discovery in the skies makes all the hard work worthwhile.

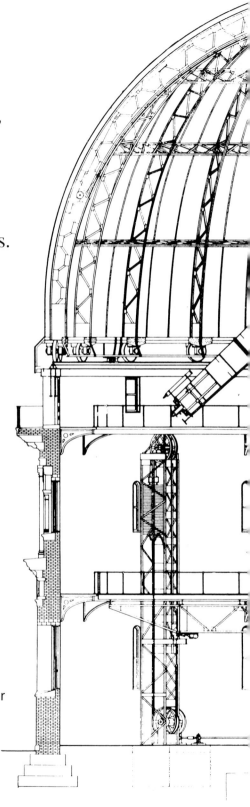

Right: Yerkes Observatory, the world's largest refracting telescope, was built in 1895 at Williams Bay, Wisconsin. *Inset, top:* An astronomer photographs the Sun in the 1920s. *Inset, bottom:* In modern times, a computer screen displays the view through a large telescope.

Opposite, top: In 1897, opticians prepared to install the 40-inch (1-m) mirror of Yerkes Observatory.

Opposite, second from top: Modern mirrors are larger, lighter, and easier to make than the Yerkes lens. Spinning furnaces are used to cast near-perfect mirrors.

Opposite, third from top: The telescope at Yerkes Observatory is used for the careful measurement of star positions.

Opposite, bottom: The 138-inch (3.5-m) Apache Point Telescope in Sunspot, New Mexico, opened in 1990. Astronomers can operate this telescope remotely by computer – without actually being at the observatory.

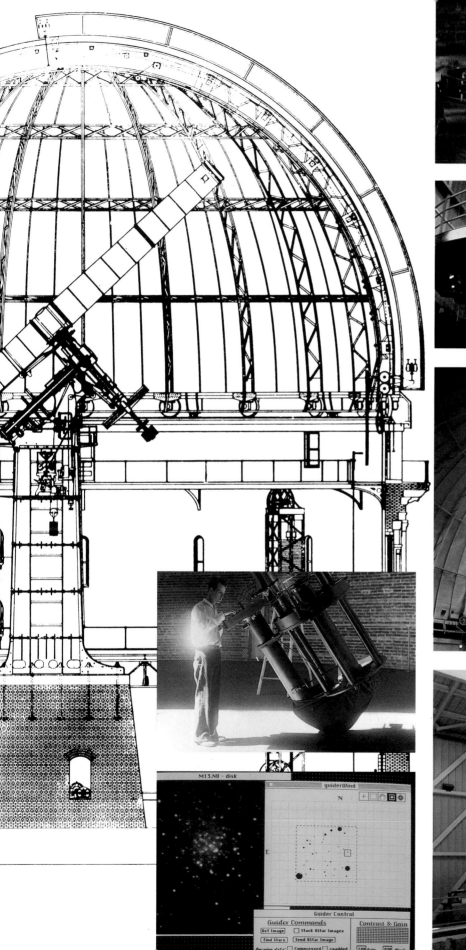

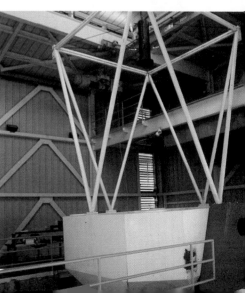

Fascinated by the Sky

Many astronomers study distant galaxies and unusual objects in remote reaches of the cosmos. But what about our Sun, the Moon, the planets, and other objects closer to home?

There is no shortage of wonderment to observe in the sky, and you do not have to be a professional astronomer to make the observations. The only requirement for the job is to be fascinated by the sky. Amateur astronomers look at the sky night after night, recording their findings, taking photographs, and drawing sketches.

Amateur astronomers are often the ones who discover new comets, observe meteors, and keep track of stars that change in brightness. Sometimes amateur astronomers even spot a nova, a star that suddenly increases significantly in brightness!

Opposite: Pictured are a star chart *(top, left)* and the plot of a star's changing brightness *(bottom).* Thousands of amateur astronomers from around the world continually contribute such observations of stellar behavior.

Opposite, top right: Leslie Peltier was called "the world's greatest nonprofessional astronomer." He discovered several comets and monitored stars that change brightness.

! Astrograms – spreading the cosmic news!

How does word get out when an astronomer spots a nova or discovers a new comet? Astronomers the world over send reports of every new astronomical discovery to telegram machines at a residence in Cambridge, Massachusetts. From there, telegrams are sent to astronomers awaiting word of the latest discoveries. Even amateurs can send and receive these "astrograms."

**TWX 710 320 6842
ASTROGRAM CAM**

BRADFIELD COMET BRADFIELD
19501 91224 79500 16190 13520
01059
20994 30769 BRADFIELD

This astrogram was sent to the Central Bureau for Astronomical Telegrams in 1950. It announces the discovery of a comet in 1949 by William Bradfield. Each word or cluster of numbers contains important data, including the name of the discoverer, the object discovered, the name of the observer, the year of the announced location in the sky *(1950)*, the date of the discovery *(91224, for 1949, December 24)*, and other details of the observation.

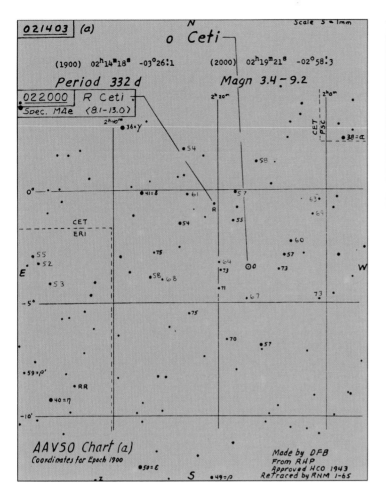

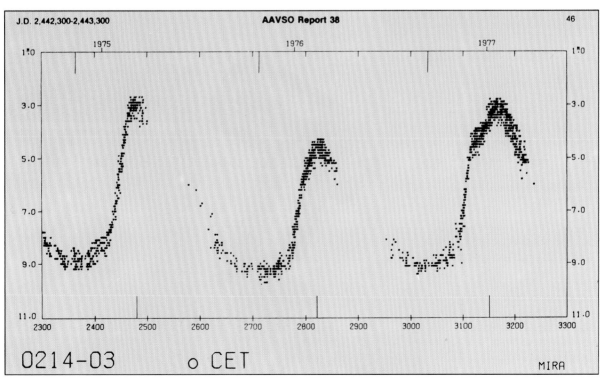

The Sky's Not the Limit

Amateur astronomers do not have the latest scientific equipment or enormous telescopes. But sometimes they can make incredible observations with just a pair of high-quality binoculars.

The amateur astronomer may have a small telescope, too. The telescope may even have a drive that makes it move in the same way the sky turns.

Some amateurs may have special cameras and computers. They may own filters that aid in observing the Sun. In addition, they often know exactly how to develop the photographs they take. Often, the best astronomical photographs – pictures of eclipses, for instance – are taken by amateurs.

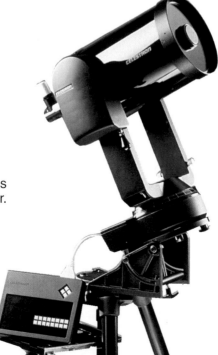

Right, center: Amateur astronomer David Kriege built this 25-inch (63.5-centimeter) telescope *(opposite and right, top)* himself. Previously, a telescope of this size would have been available only to professional astronomers in an observatory.

Right, bottom: This excellent photo of a total solar eclipse was taken by an amateur astronomer.

Immediate right: Pictured is a telescope that can be purchased from an astronomy supply store. It features a drive mechanism and a computer read-out.

Amateurs and Their Professional Work

It can be hard to tell the difference between an amateur and a professional astronomer.

One amateur, S. H. Schwabe, a German pharmacist, viewed the skies with a 2-inch (5-cm) telescope. He liked to observe the Sun, and he eventually discovered what is known as the sunspot cycle.

Asaph Hall was a carpenter who loved astronomy. He began an assistantship at the Harvard Observatory in Massachusetts and discovered the moons of Mars.

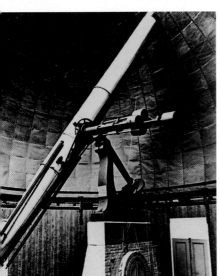

Clyde Tombaugh was too poor to go to college, but he managed to get a job as an assistant at Lowell Observatory in Arizona, where he discovered the planet Pluto!

Opposite: An artist imagines Phobos, one of the moons of Mars.

Left, top: Asaph Hall, who discovered the moons of Mars.

Left, center: The telescope Asaph Hall used to make his discoveries.

Left, bottom: Astronomer E. E. Barnard is pictured at Yerkes Observatory.

? *Eagle-eyed!*

The most eagle-eyed amateur astronomer of all may have been E. E. Barnard. In 1892, he discovered a small moon that was closer to Jupiter than any others known at the time. He could barely detect the satellite because it was so near the planet's bright light.

Barnard also told a friend about a crater he had seen on Mars. He didn't officially announce it because he thought he would be laughed at. But in 1965, a probe took pictures of Mars, and craters were revealed.

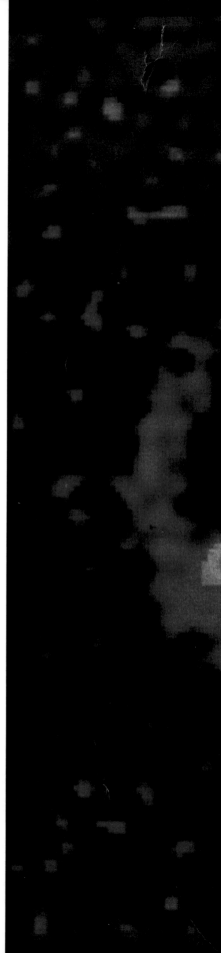

Sciences Combine in the Cosmos

Astronomy takes equipment, patience, and luck. But it also takes a lot of thinking about science and mathematics.

Albert Einstein was not an astronomer, but he developed a theory about how gravity and other forces in the Universe might work. It is called the general theory of relativity. The theory has helped astronomers in their observations of the cosmos. For instance, it has helped astronomers study unusual motions of planets and study odd things that happen to light, such as "gravitational lensing." This is the curving of light when it passes near a huge object in space.

Today, there are theories being made about how the Universe came into existence. Astronomers are trying to make observations that either prove or disprove these theories.

! Gravitational lenses – throwing astronomers a curve!

In 1936, Albert Einstein said that light from a distant star would curve around another star on its way toward Earth. Thus, the distant star would not be seen as a point of light, but as a ring of light. This ring is called a "gravitational lens" or "Einstein ring." In 1988, half a century after Einstein explained gravitational lensing, astronomers discovered that light from a quasar curves around a galaxy on its way to Earth, forming an Einstein ring.

Left: This "Einstein ring," a cosmic mirage, was created when light from a distant galaxy curved as it passed another galaxy.

Below: A sculpture of Albert Einstein in Washington, D.C. Einstein was a physicist who explained how gravity and other forces in the Universe work.

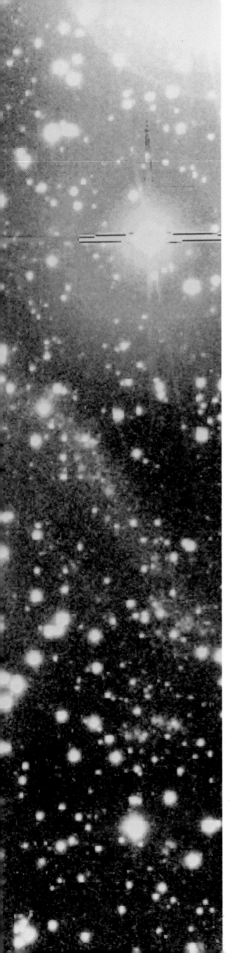

A Never-ending Quest

Despite hard work and modern technology, astronomers do not have all the answers.

New discoveries constantly remind astronomers there is still so much more to know. For example, as some astronomers were peering toward the edge of the Universe recently, their colleagues found a new galaxy, called Dwingaloo 1, only ten light-years from our own! Indeed, the Universe is full of puzzles and questions without answers.

Left: This galaxy, called Dwingaloo 1, was practically hidden behind our own Milky Way. It wasn't discovered until 1994!

Below: Just beyond Neptune's orbit lies a belt of minor planets known as the Kuiper Belt. Although astronomer Gerard Kuiper suggested, in the 1950s, that there should be such objects, none were found before 1992. In this diagram, the circular orbits of the large, outer planets are shown in blue. Kuiper Belt objects are shown as blue dots. The other orbits are from minor planets that probably wandered from the Kuiper Belt into the region of the known planets. Pluto, which may simply be the largest Kuiper Belt object of all, is also pictured as a blue dot.

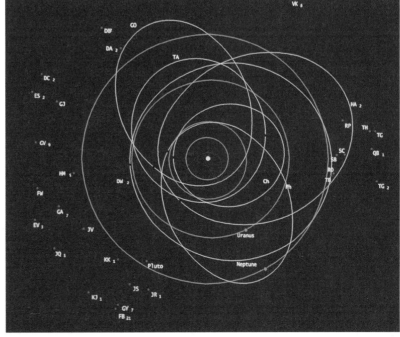

Fact File: The Spectrum

The Sun, planets, and stars are sources of visible, white light. But there is another form of visible light – the spectrum. This is light that is refracted, or broken up, into the band of colors that together make up white light. The colors of the visible spectrum can be seen through a prism and in a rainbow.

When white light is broken into its colors, information is revealed about the source of the light. For example, by examining the light of a distant galaxy with a special tool called a spectroscope, astronomers can determine whether that galaxy is moving away from Earth or toward Earth – and how fast. Light waves from a celestial body coming toward Earth are shorter, and move, or shift, toward what is called the violet end of the spectrum. Light waves from a celestial body moving away from Earth are longer, and shift toward the red end of the spectrum.

Below: White light refracted through a prism.

The Invisible Spectrum – Violet End:

Explorer 42, launched from Kenya in 1970, discovered black holes in part because of the black holes' emissions of X rays.

Cyril Hazard, an Australian astronomer, located a strong source of ultraviolet radiation with a huge red shift in 1962. This red shift indicated that the object – known as a quasar – was moving away from Earth at great speed and was at a great distance from our planet. The nearest quasars are one billion light-years away.

Johann Wilhelm Ritter (1776-1810), a German scientist, discovered ultraviolet radiation in tests performed on chemicals now used in the making of photographs.

The Visible Spectrum:

Sir Isaac Newton (1642-1727), an English scientist, refracted white light through a prism into red, orange, yellow, green, blue, and violet – the spectrum. He was the first to explain light as a pattern of bright lines of different colors.

Joseph von Fraunhofer (1787-1826), a German optician, developed a way of showing the spectrum more clearly, as a series of distinct vertical lines of color, as well as dark lines, called spectral lines. He combined the prism and the telescope into the spectroscope and used it to show that the spectral lines of the Moon and planets are the same as those of the Sun. This proved that light from the Moon and planets is, in fact, reflected sunlight.

Scientists have also learned about other types of radiation, invisible to the human eye, that exist beyond the visible radiations, or colors, of the spectrum. For example, beyond the violet end of the spectrum lie ultraviolet radiation, X rays, and gamma rays. And beyond the red end of the spectrum lie infrared radiation and radio waves.

All forms of radiation, including visible color, give off waves. These waves can be measured according to their different wavelengths. In astronomy, these wavelengths are detected with radio telescopes and other special instruments. By studying the information gathered by instruments, scientists learn about objects in deep space, such as black holes, that cannot be visited, or even seen, from Earth.

Although rockets can be sent to other worlds to collect information, astronomy is still a visual science. This means it is dependent on the gathering of light from distant sources. Because of the visible and invisible spectrum, scientists can learn about the farthest reaches of the Universe without having to actually visit those places.

Robert Wilhelm Bunsen (1824-1899) and **Gustav Robert Kirchoff** (1824-1887), German scientists, used a burner developed by and named after Bunsen to determine that certain elements give off bright or dark lines. This meant that light from a star could be analyzed to determine more than just brightness, position, and motion – but chemical makeup, as well.

Armand H. L. Fizeau (1819-1896), a French scientist, used a spectroscope in 1848 to show whether an object is moving toward Earth (violet shift) or away from Earth (red shift) – and how fast.

Annie Jump Cannon (1863-1941), an American astronomer, used spectrographic methods to classify stars in order of decreasing temperature.

Wilhelm Wien (1864-1928), a German scientist, used the spectrum to measure star temperatures.

Vesto Melvin Slipher (1875-1969), an American astronomer, discovered that most galaxies show a red shift, meaning they are moving away from Earth. This discovery contributed to the "Big Bang" theory of the birth of the Universe.

The Invisible Spectrum – Red End:

William Herschel (1738-1822), a German-born English astronomer, discovered infrared radiation by measuring heat beyond the red end of the spectrum and getting a higher temperature reading. This led to the conclusion that there must be a line beyond red – infrared – that cannot be seen.

Heinrich Rudolph Hertz (1857-1894), a German scientist, detected wavelengths much longer than infrared radiation – radio waves.

Karl Guthe Jansky (1905-1950), an American radio engineer, detected a radio "hiss" coming from the center of our Galaxy. His discovery led to the birth of radio astronomy.

Jocelyn Bell Burnell, a British astronomer, detected rapid pulses of radio waves from a star in 1967. She discovered rapidly spinning, densely packed neutron stars, or pulsars.

More Books about Astronomy

Asimov on Astronomy. Asimov (Doubleday)
Astro-Dome Book: 3-D Map of the Night Sky. Hunig (Constellation)
Astronomy Basics. Litpak (Prentice-Hall)
Astronomy in Ancient Times. Asimov (Gareth Stevens)
Discovering the Stars. Santrey (Troll)
Eyes on the Universe: The History of the Telescope. Asimov (Houghton Mifflin)
Night Sky. Barrett (Franklin Watts)
A Stargazer's Guide. Asimov (Gareth Stevens)

Videos

Astronomy Today. (Gareth Stevens)
Space Spotter's Guide. (Gareth Stevens)

Places to Visit

You can explore the Universe without leaving Earth. Here are some museums and centers where you can find a variety of space exhibits.

International Women's Air and
    Space Museum
1 Chamber Plaza
Dayton, OH 45402

Edmonton Space and Science Centre
11211 - 142nd Street
Edmonton, Alberta K5M 4A1

The Space and Rocket Center
    and Space Camp
One Tranquility Base
Huntsville, AL 35807

Perth Observatory
Walnut Road
Bickley, W.A. 6076
Australia

Seneca College Planetarium
1750 Finch Avenue East
North York, Ontario M2J 2X5

Palomar Observatory
35899 Canfield Road
Palomar Mountain, CA 92060

Places to Write

Here are some places you can write for more information about astronomy. Be sure to state what kind of information you would like. Include your full name and address so they can write back to you.

National Space Society
922 Pennsylvania Avenue SE
Washington, D.C. 20003

Canadian Space Agency
Communications Department
6767 Route de L'Aeroport
Saint Hubert, Quebec J3Y 8Y9

Sydney Observatory
P. O. Box K346
Haymarket 2000 Australia

NASA Lewis Research Center
Educational Services Office
21000 Brookpark Road
Cleveland, OH 44135

Glossary

amateur: a person who engages in an art, science, or sport for enjoyment rather than profit.

astronomy: the study of various celestial bodies in the Universe.

atmosphere: the gases that surround a planet, star, or moon.

billion: the number represented by 1 followed by nine zeroes – 1,000,000,000. In some countries, this number is called "a thousand million." In these countries, one billion would then be represented by 1 followed by twelve zeroes – 1,000,000,000,000 – a million million.

black hole: a massive object – usually a collapsed star – so tightly packed that not even light can escape the force of its gravity.

calendar: a system for dividing time, most commonly into days, weeks, and months.

comet: an object in space made of ice, rock, and gas. It has a vapor tail that may be seen when the comet's orbit brings it close to the Sun.

crater: a hole or pit on a planet or moon created by volcanic explosions or the impact of meteorites.

galaxy: any of the many large groupings of stars, gas, and dust that exist in the Universe. Our Galaxy is known as the Milky Way.

infrared radiation: infrared is a form of invisible light, but it cannot be felt as heat.

nova: a star that suddenly increases greatly in brightness and returns to its original appearance in a few weeks, months, or years.

orbit: the path that one celestial object follows as it circles, or revolves, around another.

probe: a craft that travels in space, photographing celestial bodies and even landing on some of them.

pulsar: a neutron star that sends out rapid pulses of light or other radiation.

quasar: a starlike core of a galaxy that may have a large black hole at its center.

radio telescope: an instrument that uses a radio receiver and antenna both to see into space and to listen for messages from space.

radio waves: electromagnetic waves that can be detected by radio-receiving equipment.

sunspot: a dark area on the Sun caused by gases that are cooler and shine less brightly than hot gases.

supernova: the result of a huge star exploding. When a supernova occurs, material from the star is spread through space.

telescope: an instrument with lenses or mirrors for the purpose of detecting objects in space.

Universe: all existing things, including Earth, the Sun, the entire Solar System, galaxies, and all that is or may be beyond.

Index

Born in 1920, Isaac Asimov came to the United States as a young boy from his native Russia. As a young man, he was a student of biochemistry. In time, he became one of the most productive writers the world has ever known. His books cover a spectrum of topics, including science, history, language theory, fantasy, and science fiction. His brilliant imagination gained him the respect and admiration of adults and children alike. Sadly, Isaac Asimov died shortly after the publication of the first edition of *Isaac Asimov's Library of the Universe*.

The publishers wish to thank the following for permission to reproduce copyright material: front cover, Jet Propulsion Laboratory; 4 (upper), Collection of George G. Young; 4 (lower), Courtesy of Wyoming Travel Commission; 5 (large), © Greg Mort 1984; 6 (upper), © W. M. Keck Observatory/Andrew Perala; 6 (lower), © W. M. Keck Observatory/Caltech; 7 (upper), Courtesy of Itek Optical Systems, in conjunction with the California Association for Research in Astronomy; 7 (lower), © California Institute of Technology; 8 (upper and center), NASA/STScI; 8 (lower), © Fred Klein; 9, NASA/STScI; 10, © Mark Maxwell 1988; 11 (upper left), Jet Propulsion Laboratory; 11 (center left), Science Photo Libraries; 11 (lower left), NOAO; 11 (lower right), © Royal Observatory, Edinburgh 1986; 12 (both), 13 (both), © NRAO/AUI; 14-15, NOAO; 15 (large), Courtesy of Joe Stancampiano, Karl Luttrell, and the IMB Collaboration; 15 (inset), Courtesy of the IMB Collaboration; 16-17, 17 (left, both), (upper right, second, and lower right), Yerkes Observatory; 17 (right, third), © Leslie Bellavance 1989; 19 (upper left and lower), printed with special permission of Dr. Janet A. Mattei, Director of AAVSO; 19 (upper right), © Don Hurless; 20 (left), Courtesy of Celestron International; 20 (upper right), 20-21, Matthew Groshek and Kate Kriege/© Gareth Stevens, Inc. 1989; 20 (lower right), NASA; 22, © Joe Schabram 1987; 23 (upper and center), US Navy; 23 (lower), Yerkes Observatory; 24-25, © NRAO/AUI; 25, Courtesy of the National Academy of Sciences; 26-27, Dwingaloo Obscured Galaxy Survey team, S. Hughes, & S. Maddox/Isaac Newton Telescope (RGO); 27, Courtesy Gareth Williams, Minor Planet Center; 28, Matthew Groshek/© Gareth Stevens, Inc. 1989.